spot

MIGHTY MACHINES

TANKS

by Wendy Strobel Dieker

AMICUS | AMICUS INK

hull

tracks

Look for these words and pictures as you read.

hatch

main gun

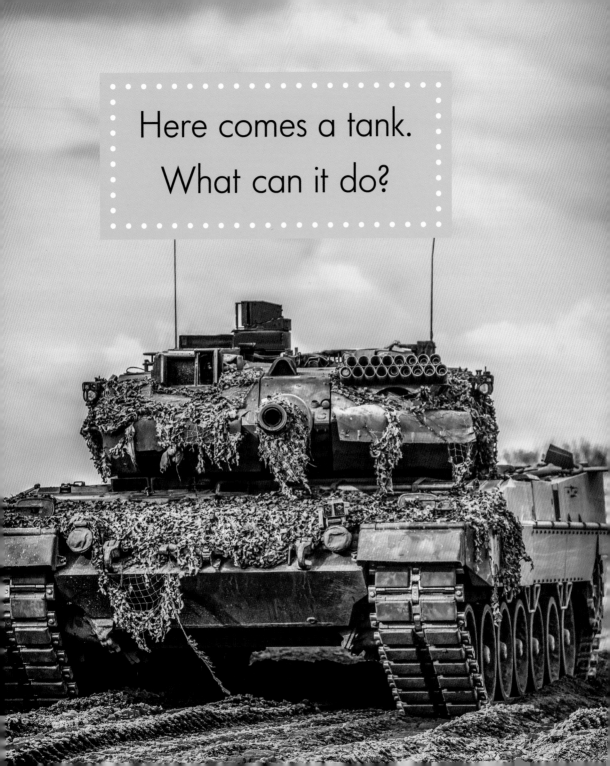

Here comes a tank.
What can it do?

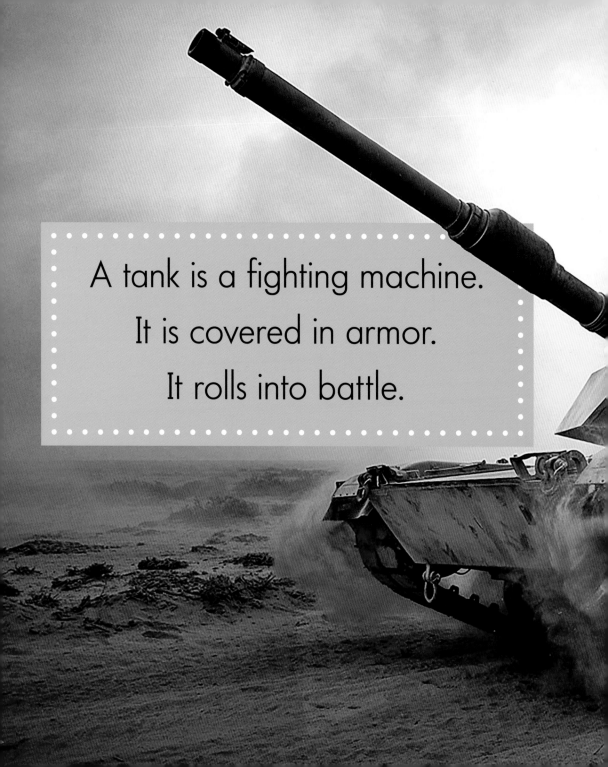

A tank is a fighting machine.
It is covered in armor.
It rolls into battle.

See the hull?
The crew is inside.
They stay safe.

hull

See the tracks?

They roll over rough ground.

They roll through mud.

tracks

hatch

See the hatch?

The driver looks out.

Where is the enemy?

See the main gun?
It shoots farther than 1 mile
(1.6 km). Boom! It's a hit!

main gun

The tank moves on.
It is ready for the next fight.

See the hull?
The crew is inside.
They stay safe.

hull

See the tracks?
They roll over rough ground.
They roll through mud.

tracks

hull

tracks

Did you find?

hatch

main gun

hatch

See the hatch?
The driver looks out.
Where is the enemy?

See the main gun?
It shoots farther than 1 mile
(1.6 km). Boom! It's a hit!

main gun

Spot is published by Amicus and Amicus Ink
P.O. Box 1329, Mankato, MN 56002
www.amicuspublishing.us

Library of Congress Cataloging-in-Publication Data
Names: Dieker, Wendy Strobel, author.
Title: Tanks / by Wendy Strobel Dieker.
Description: Mankato, Minnesota : Amicus, [2020] | Series:
 Spot. Mighty machines | Audience: K to grade 3.
Identifiers: LCCN 2018024632 (print) | LCCN 2018036468
 (ebook) | ISBN 9781681517308 (pdf) | ISBN
 9781681516486 (binding) | ISBN 9781681524344 (pbk.)
Subjects: LCSH: Tanks (Military science)--Juvenile literature.|
 Tanks (Military science)--Parts--Juvenile literature. |
 CYAC: Tanks (Military science) | LCGFT: Instructional and
 educational works. | Picture books. Classification: LCC
 UG446.5 (ebook) | LCC UG446.5 .D5225 2020 (print) |
 DDC 623.74/752--dc23 LC record available at https://lccn.
 loc.gov/2018024632

Printed in China

HC 10 9 8 7 6 5 4 3 2 1
PB 10 9 8 7 6 5 4 3 2 1

Alissa Thielges, editor
Deb Miner, series designer
Aubrey Harper, book designer
Holly Young, photo researcher

Photos by StockTrek/Terry Moore
cover, 16; iStock/vasiliki 1; iStock/
huettenhoelscher 3; defense.gov
4–5; Dvids/U.S. Marine Corps photo
by Pfc. Beard or Cpl. Andre Heath
6–7; Dvids/U.S. Marine Corps Photo
by Cpl. Alexander Sturdivant 8–9;
WikiCommons/U.S. Army photo by Sgt.
Aaron Ellerman 10–11; WikiCommons/
Sgt Devin Nichols 12–13; Alamy/PJF
Military Collection 14–15

TANKS